Little **BIG** Chats

Private Parts are Private

by Jayneen Sanders

illustrated by Cherie Zamazing

Private Parts are Private
Educate2Empower Publishing an imprint of
UpLoad Publishing Pty Ltd
Victoria Australia
www.upload.com.au

First published in 2021

Written by Jayneen Sanders
Illustrations by Cherie Zamazing

Jayneen Sanders asserts her right to be identified as the author of this work.
Cherie Zamazing asserts her right to be identified as the illustrator of this work.

Designed by Stephanie Spartels, Studio Spartels

ISBN: 9781761160257 (hbk) 9781761160110 (pbk)

NATIONAL
LIBRARY
OF AUSTRALIA

A catalogue record for this
book is available from the
National Library of Australia

Disclaimer: The information in this book is advice only, written by the author based on
her advocacy in this area, and her experience working with children as a classroom teacher
and mother. The information is not meant to be a substitute for professional advice. If you
are concerned about a child's behavior seek professional help.

Using Little BIG Chats

The *Little BIG Chats* series has been written to assist parents, caregivers and educators to have open and age-appropriate conversations with young children around crucial, and yet at times, 'tough' topics. And what better way than using children's picture books! Some pages will have questions for your child to interact with and discuss. Feel free to use these questions and the Discussion Questions provided on page 19 of this book to help you assist your child with the topic being explored. Stop at any time to unpack the text together; and try to follow your child's lead wherever that conversation may take you! So, please, get comfy and start some empowering 'chats' around some BIG topics with your child.

The Body Safety titles should ideally be read in the following order:
Consent, *My Safety Network*, *My Early Warning Signs*,
Private Parts are Private, and *Secrets and Surprises*.
The remaining titles can be read in any order.

Meet the

Little BIG Chats
KIDS

Theodore

Asha

Ardie

Tom

Jun

Jamie

Belle

Lisa

Maisy

Tilly

Maya

Ben

Hi! I'm Ben.
Today we're learning
that our private parts
are private.

Private means just for you.

Your private parts are the parts of your body under your bathing suit or underwear.

You should always use
the correct names for
your private parts.

Boys have a penis,
testicles and a bottom.

Girls have a vulva on
the outside and a vagina
on the inside. They also
have nipples and a bottom.

When girls get older,
the area around their
nipples grows into breasts.

Your mouth is a private part too.

ALL About our BODIES

No one should touch
your private parts.

They belong to only you.

When you were a baby,
your parents washed and
dried your private parts.

Now that you are older,
you can wash and dry
your own private parts.

If someone does touch your private parts or asks you to touch their private parts or shows you pictures of private parts you can say, 'Stop! This is my body!'

Then tell a trusted grown-up on your Safety Network straightaway.

WHO ARE THE GROWN-UPS ON YOUR SAFETY NETWORK?

If you feel scared
and it's hard to say,
'Stop! This is my body!'
get away as quickly
as you can.

Then tell a trusted
grown-up on your
Safety Network
straightaway.

They will listen to you
and they will help you.

MAMA
DAD
MR PETERS
GRANNY
MY SAFETY NETWORK

15

Sometimes if you are sick,
a doctor might need to check or
even touch your private parts.

This is only okay if a grown-up
from your Safety Network is
with you.

The doctor should always
ask for your consent first.

Remember!

You are the boss of your body!
What you say goes!

WHO IS THE
BOSS OF
YOUR BODY?

18

DISCUSSION QUESTIONS
for Parents, Caregivers and Educators

The following Discussion Questions are intended as a guide, and can be used to initiate open, age-appropriate and empowering conversations with your child.

This book reinforces the correct anatomical names children and adults should use for the private parts; and teaches children what they should do if they are touched inappropriately.

Page 5
Introduce Ben. Ask, 'What do you think "private" means?' Say, 'That's right! Private means just for you.' Ask, 'What might be some private places in our home/school?' Say, 'The spaces that are shared by everyone are called public spaces.' Ask, 'What might be some public spaces?'

Pages 6-7
Ask, 'Where are your private parts?'

Pages 8-9
Ask, 'Can you remember the correct names for the private parts?' Note: if you are uncomfortable using the correct terms, your child will be too. Use the correct names with your child. Say, 'You have a nose, arms, fingers and toes and you have a penis/vulva.' Note: for a child who may be going through gender questioning, you could read the text as: 'Some children have...' so they feel included.

Pages 10-11
Ask, 'Who do your private parts belong to?' Note: we do not want children growing up ashamed of their private parts. As the discussion progresses, reassure your child that they can touch their own private parts but only in a private place such as the bathroom or bedroom (if it is not shared with a sibling). Children touching their genitals is normal and feels good; it is only when it is excessive that advice from a health professional may be required.

Pages 12-13
Together with your child practice standing in a superhero pose and placing your hand out (as Ben is doing) and say, 'Stop! This is my body'. Review with your child who is on their Safety Network, and what to do if they are touched inappropriately, asked to touch someone inappropriately or are shown images of private parts. To review the Safety Network concept, see the title 'My Safety Network' included in the Little BIG Chats series.

Pages 14-15
Note: as with many adults when touched inappropriately, children may freeze. Tell your child that if they feel scared or threatened in any way, the MOST important thing is for them to get away as safely and as quickly as they can, and to tell a grown-up on their Safety Network straightaway. Also reinforce that if an adult, an older child or another child touches them in an unsafe way, it is never ever their fault.

Pages 16-17
Ask, 'What do you think consent means?' A simple definition could be: 'People have to ask me before coming inside my body boundary.' To review consent, see the title 'Consent' included in the Little BIG Chats series.

Page 18
Have your child shout loud and proud, 'I am the boss of my body! What I say goes!'

For more books that cover Body Safety skills in depth, see Jayneen Sanders' children's books 'No Means No!'; 'My Body! What I Say Goes!'; 'Let's Talk About Body Boundaries, Consent and Respect'; 'ABC of Body Safety and Consent' and 'Some Secrets Should Never Be Kept'.

Little BIG Chats

A series of 12 little books to help kids unpack BIG topics

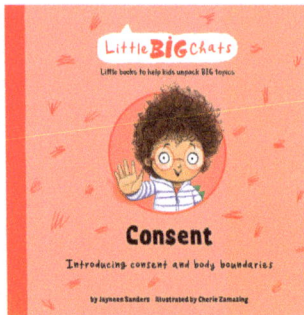

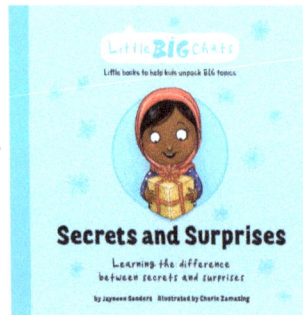

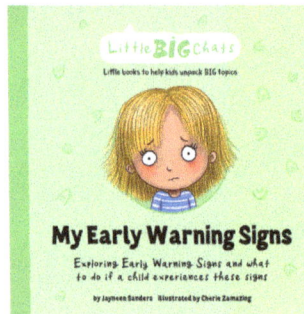

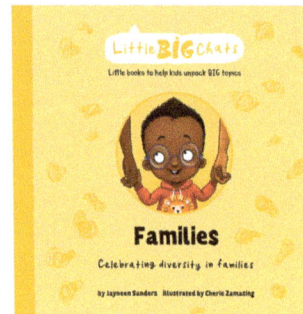

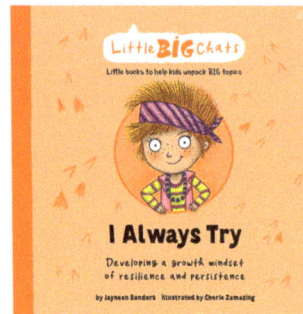

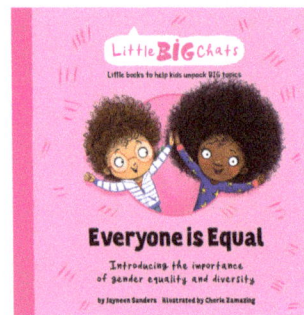

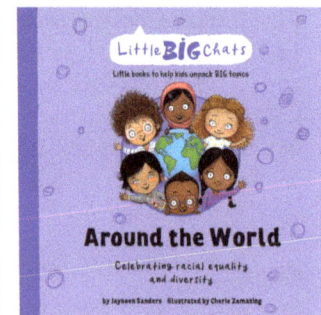

Little BIG Chats
Little books to help kids unpack BIG topics

Consent
Introducing consent and body boundaries
by Jayneen Sanders   Illustrated by Cherie Zamazing

Little BIG Chats
Little books to help kids unpack BIG topics

Secrets and Surprises
Learning the difference between secrets and surprises
by Jayneen Sanders   Illustrated by Cherie Zamazing

Little BIG Chats
Little books to help kids unpack BIG topics

Private Parts are Private
Learning private parts are private and what to do if touched inappropriately
by Jayneen Sanders   Illustrated by Cherie Zamazing

Little BIG Chats
Little books to help kids unpack BIG topics

My Safety Network
Introducing a Safety Network (3 to 5 trusted adults a child can go to if they feel unsafe)
by Jayneen Sanders   Illustrated by Cherie Zamazing

Little BIG Chats
Little books to help kids unpack BIG topics

My Early Warning Signs
Exploring Early Warning Signs and what to do if a child experiences these signs
by Jayneen Sanders   Illustrated by Cherie Zamazing

Little BIG Chats
Little books to help kids unpack BIG topics

Families
Celebrating diversity in families
by Jayneen Sanders   Illustrated by Cherie Zamazing

Little BIG Chats
Little books to help kids unpack BIG topics

I Always Try
Developing a growth mindset of resilience and persistence
by Jayneen Sanders   Illustrated by Cherie Zamazing

Little BIG Chats
Little books to help kids unpack BIG topics

Feelings
Understanding different feelings and emotions
by Jayneen Sanders   Illustrated by Cherie Zamazing

Little BIG Chats
Little books to help kids unpack BIG topics

Everyone is Equal
Introducing the importance of gender equality and diversity
by Jayneen Sanders   Illustrated by Cherie Zamazing

Little BIG Chats
Little books to help kids unpack BIG topics

Empathy
Exploring the meaning of empathy and kindness
by Jayneen Sanders   Illustrated by Cherie Zamazing

Little BIG Chats
Little books to help kids unpack BIG topics

Mindfulness
Exploring the importance of mindfulness and learning calming skills
by Jayneen Sanders   Illustrated by Cherie Zamazing

Little BIG Chats
Little books to help kids unpack BIG topics

Around the World
Celebrating racial equality and diversity
by Jayneen Sanders   Illustrated by Cherie Zamazing

www.ingramcontent.com/pod-product-compliance
Lightning Source LLC
Chambersburg PA
CBHW040002040426
42337CB00032B/5202